HERE'S HOW IT WORKS

BUY A JOURNAL

Buy a journal & register it online. This ensures that you will receive it back once all 12 Acts have been completed.

PASS IT ON

Complete the very first Act of Good for someone & give them the journal. (Yes, literally releasing it into the world.)

FOLLOW ITS JOURNEY

Follow along as it is passed from one person to the next, collecting the stories of where it goes, what it does and the lives touched along the way.

GET IT BACK

After all 12 Acts have been completed, the journal is returned to you to be kept as a reminder of how you made the world a better place!

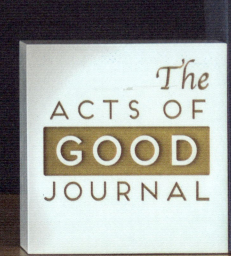

Created by: Adam Benton
Published by: Inspire Good Publishing Co.

(left) "The Acts Of Good Journal"
original concept sketch &
author Adam Benton

When I started this book, I simply hoped to "inspire good in the world." I didn't know what that really meant then, and I honestly still don't fully understand what that means today. However, the experiences and outcomes from this project continue to teach me unimaginable life lessons of beauty, love and kindness.

As you experience your own personal journey with this journal, here are a few lessons (truths / facts) that I have learned that I hope empower you to not only complete your Act of Good, but inspire you in your everyday life.

1. You already contain all of the power within you to give good (Don't hesitate, have confidence).

2. The size, effort or value of an Act of Good is irrelevant because it is the "ACTION OF GOOD" that impacts life.

3. What appears to be a molehill to you could be Mt. Everest to someone else (Don't underestimate your abilities).

4. No matter what you do in whatever capacity, remember that you are about to blindside someone with the acknowledgment that they are thought of, cared for, accepted, noticed, remarkable and loved, and <u>that</u> "Act" may contain unimaginable outcomes.

5. The most powerful Acts of Good won't be found in this journal, they will be much smaller cultural changes imbedded in our daily lives (Smiling more, saying the compliment you are thinking, giving more high-fives).

You are the good in the world. Thank you for being a part of this journal and making the world a better place.

-AB

ACT
1

YOU ARE THE OWNER OF THIS JOURNAL

HERE'S HOW IT WORKS

This journal is yours to release into the world with the first Act of Good. It will be passed from one person to the next through continued Acts of Good, capturing the stories of where it goes, what it does and the lives touched along the way. After all 12 Acts have been completed, this journal will be mailed back to you to be kept as a reminder of how you made the world a better place.

Follow the steps below to complete the first Act of Good:

STEP 1

STEP 2

STEP 3

REGISTER THIS JOURNAL

WRITE IN THE JOURNAL

PASS IT ON!

Go to: **ActsOfGood.com** and register this journal. This allows you to track the journal after you pass it on, and it's the only way you will receive it back once all of the Acts have been completed.

On the next page, tell us a little about yourself and what you hope this journal will accomplish.

Complete the first Act of Good for someone, and give them this journal. How you choose to do so is up to you. Don't let rules, zip codes or actions limit your creativity.

(VISIT ActsOfGood.com IF YOU HAVE ANY QUESTIONS ABOUT HOW THIS WORKS)

TELL US ABOUT YOURSELF

M F
CIRCLE ONE
SEX

WRITE HERE
AGE

WHAT IS TODAY'S DATE?

_____ / _____ / _____
(MONTH)   (DAY)   (YEAR)

WHERE ARE YOU CURRENTLY IN THE WORLD?

_____ / _____ / _____
(CITY)   (STATE)   (COUNTRY)

WHO DO YOU LOOK UP TO, AND WHY?
(PUBLIC FIGURE, SOMEONE YOU KNOW...)

_____

_____

_____

WHAT ARE YOUR GRANDPARENTS' ETHNICITIES?
(WE ASK THESE QUESTIONS ONLY TO CELEBRATE DIVERSITY, BUT FEEL FREE TO SKIP IF YOU DON'T FEEL LIKE ANSWERING.)

_____   _____
(DAD'S DAD)   (DAD'S MOM)

_____   _____
(MOM'S DAD)   (MOM'S MOM)

TELL US ABOUT
YOUR EXPERIENCE

IS THERE AN ORGANIZATION THAT INSPIRES YOU?

_____
(ORGANIZATION NAME)
_____
(WHAT THEY DO)
_____
_____
_____
_____
(WEBSITE URL)

WHAT DO YOU HOPE THIS JOURNAL WILL ACCOMPLISH?

_____
_____
_____
_____
_____
_____
_____
_____

(IT'S TIME TO PASS IT ON)

On the next page, decide who will receive your Act of Good and what you want to do for them.

WHO
WILL RECEIVE YOUR ACT OF GOOD?

It's time to decide who will receive your Act of Good. Choosing who you are going to do your Act of Good for makes deciding what you are going to do much easier.

- NEIGHBOR
- FRIEND
- STRANGER
- TEACHER
- CO-WORKER
- FAMILY MEMBER
- NEW ACQUAINTANCE
- _____ (OTHER)

(ONCE YOU DECIDE...)
TELL US WHY YOU CHOSE THIS PERSON

_____
_____
_____
_____

WHAT
ARE YOU GOING TO DO FOR THEM?

Explore the thoughts and questions below as you start to define / plan your Act Of Good. Remember that this is about making the person feel thought of, cared for, loved, noticed, remarkable, and accepted, so let that be your inspiration.

- Focus your thoughts on the person you chose.
- Reflect on your past conversations.
- What makes them smile?
- What do they enjoy?
- Do they have any wants, needs or goals?
- Would your time, talent or ability help them?
- Is it an activity?
- Is it a gift?
- Have you decided?
- Turn the page for final instructions on how to pass it on.

IT'S TIME TO DO THE 1ST ACT OF GOOD AND PASS IT ON.

Put the bookmark on the opening page of the next Act of Good before you give them the journal.

Look up your journal from time to time at ActsOfGood.com to find out where it is.

THANK YOU FOR BEING A PART OF THIS JOURNAL AND MAKING THE WORLD A BETTER PLACE!

SHARE YOUR EXPERIENCE

ACT

2

YOU ARE THE 2ND PERSON TO RECEIVE THIS JOURNAL

HERE'S HOW IT WORKS

This journal has been released into the world to create and inspire Acts of Good. Each journal is passed from one person to the next through an Act of Good, capturing the stories of where it goes, what it does and the lives touched along the way. It could have been given to millions of other people, yet here it lies in your hands. After all 12 Acts have been completed, this journal will be returned to its owner to share the stories of how you made the world a better place.

Follow the steps below to complete the next Act of Good:

STEP 1 — **CHECK-IN THIS JOURNAL**

Go to: **ActsOfGood.com** and check this journal in. This lets everyone know where it is and allows you to track / follow where it goes after you pass it on.

(YOU CAN FIND THIS JOURNAL # IN THE FRONT OF THE BOOK)

STEP 2 — **WRITE IN THE JOURNAL**

Over the next few pages, tell us a little about yourself and your experience.

STEP 3 — **PASS IT ON!**

Complete the second Act of Good for someone, and give them this journal. How you choose to do so is up to you. Don't let rules, zip codes or actions limit your creativity.

(VISIT ActsOfGood.com IF YOU HAVE ANY QUESTIONS ABOUT HOW THIS WORKS)

TELL US ABOUT YOURSELF

M F
CIRCLE ONE
SEX

WRITE HERE
AGE

WHAT IS TODAY'S DATE?

_____ / _____ / _____
(MONTH)   (DAY)   (YEAR)

WHERE ARE YOU CURRENTLY IN THE WORLD?

_____ / _____ / _____
(CITY)   (STATE)   (COUNTRY)

WHAT ARE 3 THINGS THAT MAKE YOU THE HAPPIEST?

1. _____
2. _____
3. _____

HOW DO YOU DEFINE YOUR RELIGION?
(WE ASK THESE QUESTIONS ONLY TO CELEBRATE DIVERSITY, BUT FEEL FREE TO SKIP IF YOU DON'T FEEL LIKE ANSWERING.)

_____

_____

TELL US ABOUT YOUR EXPERIENCE

WHAT ACT OF GOOD WAS DONE FOR YOU?

_____
_____
_____
_____
_____
_____
_____
_____

HOW DID THIS IMPACT / AFFECT YOU?

_____
_____
_____
_____
_____
_____
_____

(IT'S TIME TO PASS IT ON)

On the next page, decide who will receive your Act of Good and what you want to do for them.

WHO
WILL RECEIVE YOUR ACT OF GOOD?

It's time to decide who will receive your Act of Good. Choosing who you are going to do your Act of Good for makes deciding what you are going to do much easier.

- NEIGHBOR
- FRIEND
- STRANGER
- TEACHER
- CO-WORKER
- FAMILY MEMBER
- NEW ACQUAINTANCE
- _____ (OTHER)

(ONCE YOU DECIDE...)
TELL US WHY YOU CHOSE THIS PERSON

_____
_____
_____
_____

WHAT
ARE YOU GOING TO DO FOR THEM?

Explore the thoughts and questions below as you start to define / plan your Act Of Good. Remember that this is about making the person feel thought of, cared for, loved, noticed, remarkable, and accepted, so let that be your inspiration.

- Focus your thoughts on the person you chose.
- Reflect on your past conversations.
- What makes them smile?
- What do they enjoy?
- Do they have any wants, needs or goals?
- Would your time, talent or ability help them?
- Is it an activity?
- Is it a gift?
- Have you decided?
- Turn the page for final instructions on how to pass it on.

IT'S TIME TO DO THE 2ND ACT OF GOOD AND PASS IT ON.

Put the bookmark on the opening page of the next Act of Good before you give them the journal.

Look up this journal from time to time at ActsOfGood.com to find out where it is.

THANK YOU FOR BEING A PART OF THIS JOURNAL AND MAKING THE WORLD A BETTER PLACE!

SHARE YOUR EXPERIENCE

ACT 3

YOU ARE THE 3RD PERSON TO RECEIVE THIS JOURNAL

HERE'S HOW IT WORKS

This journal has been released into the world to create and inspire Acts of Good. Each journal is passed from one person to the next through an Act of Good, capturing the stories of where it goes, what it does and the lives touched along the way. It could have been given to millions of other people, yet here it lies in your hands. After all 12 Acts have been completed, this journal will be returned to its owner to share the stories of how you made the world a better place.

Follow the steps below to complete the next Act of Good:

STEP 1

CHECK-IN THIS JOURNAL

Go to: **ActsOfGood.com** and check this journal in. This lets everyone know where it is and allows you to track / follow where it goes after you pass it on.

(YOU CAN FIND THIS JOURNAL # IN THE FRONT OF THE BOOK)

STEP 2

WRITE IN THE JOURNAL

Over the next few pages, tell us a little about yourself and your experience.

STEP 3

PASS IT ON!

Complete the third Act of Good for someone, and give them this journal. How you choose to do so is up to you. Don't let rules, zip codes or actions limit your creativity.

(VISIT ActsOfGood.com IF YOU HAVE ANY QUESTIONS ABOUT HOW THIS WORKS)

TELL US ABOUT YOURSELF

M F
CIRCLE ONE
SEX

WRITE HERE
AGE

WHAT IS TODAY'S DATE?

_____ / _____ / _____
(MONTH)   (DAY)   (YEAR)

WHERE ARE YOU CURRENTLY IN THE WORLD?

_____ / _____ / _____
(CITY)   (STATE)   (COUNTRY)

WHAT'S A "LOCAL" __(ANYTHING)__ PEOPLE SHOULD KNOW ABOUT?
(AND WHY?)

_____
_____
_____

HOW DO YOU DEFINE YOUR POLITICAL AFFILIATION?
(WE ASK THESE QUESTIONS ONLY TO CELEBRATE DIVERSITY, BUT FEEL FREE TO SKIP IF YOU DON'T FEEL LIKE ANSWERING.)

_____
_____

TELL US ABOUT YOUR EXPERIENCE

WHAT ACT OF GOOD WAS DONE FOR YOU?

_____
_____
_____
_____
_____
_____
_____
_____

HOW DID THIS IMPACT / AFFECT YOU?

_____
_____
_____
_____
_____
_____
_____

(IT'S TIME TO PASS IT ON)

On the next page, decide who will receive your Act of Good and what you want to do for them.

WHO
WILL RECEIVE YOUR ACT OF GOOD?

It's time to decide who will receive your Act of Good. Choosing who you are going to do your Act of Good for makes deciding what you are going to do much easier.

- NEIGHBOR
- FRIEND
- STRANGER
- TEACHER
- CO-WORKER
- FAMILY MEMBER
- NEW ACQUAINTANCE
- _____ (OTHER)

(ONCE YOU DECIDE...)
TELL US WHY YOU CHOSE THIS PERSON

_____
_____
_____
_____

WHAT
ARE YOU GOING TO DO FOR THEM?

Explore the thoughts and questions below as you start to define / plan your Act Of Good. Remember that this is about making the person feel thought of, cared for, loved, noticed, remarkable, and accepted, so let that be your inspiration.

- Focus your thoughts on the person you chose.
- Reflect on your past conversations.
- What makes them smile?
- What do they enjoy?
- Do they have any wants, needs or goals?
- Would your time, talent or ability help them?
- Is it an activity?
- Is it a gift?
- Have you decided?
- Turn the page for final instructions on how to pass it on.

IT'S TIME TO DO THE 3RD ACT OF GOOD AND PASS IT ON.

Put the bookmark on the opening page of the next Act of Good before you give them the journal.

Look up this journal from time to time at ActsOfGood.com to find out where it is.

THANK YOU FOR BEING A PART OF THIS JOURNAL AND MAKING THE WORLD A BETTER PLACE!

SHARE YOUR EXPERIENCE

ACT
4

YOU ARE THE 4TH PERSON TO RECEIVE THIS JOURNAL

HERE'S HOW IT WORKS

This journal has been released into the world to create and inspire Acts of Good. Each journal is passed from one person to the next through an Act of Good, capturing the stories of where it goes, what it does and the lives touched along the way. It could have been given to millions of other people, yet here it lies in your hands. After all 12 Acts have been completed, this journal will be returned to its owner to share the stories of how you made the world a better place.

Follow the steps below to complete the next Act of Good:

STEP 1

STEP 2

STEP 3

CHECK-IN THIS JOURNAL

WRITE IN THE JOURNAL

PASS IT ON!

Go to: **ActsOfGood.com** and check this journal in. This lets everyone know where it is and allows you to track / follow where it goes after you pass it on.

(YOU CAN FIND THIS JOURNAL # IN THE FRONT OF THE BOOK)

Over the next few pages, tell us a little about yourself and your experience.

Complete the fourth Act of Good for someone, and give them this journal. How you choose to do so is up to you. Don't let rules, zip codes or actions limit your creativity.

(VISIT ActsOfGood.com IF YOU HAVE ANY QUESTIONS ABOUT HOW THIS WORKS)

TELL US ABOUT YOURSELF

M F
CIRCLE ONE
SEX

WRITE HERE
AGE

WHAT IS TODAY'S DATE?

_____ / _____ / _____
(MONTH)   (DAY)   (YEAR)

WHERE ARE YOU CURRENTLY IN THE WORLD?

_____ / _____ / _____
(CITY)   (STATE)   (COUNTRY)

WHO DO YOU LOOK UP TO, AND WHY?
(PUBLIC FIGURE, SOMEONE YOU KNOW...)

_____
_____
_____

WHAT ARE YOUR GRANDPARENTS' ETHNICITIES?
(WE ASK THESE QUESTIONS ONLY TO CELEBRATE DIVERSITY, BUT FEEL FREE TO SKIP IF YOU DON'T FEEL LIKE ANSWERING.)

_____   _____
(DAD'S DAD)   (DAD'S MOM)

_____   _____
(MOM'S DAD)   (MOM'S MOM)

TELL US ABOUT YOUR EXPERIENCE

WHAT ACT OF GOOD WAS DONE FOR YOU?

_____
_____
_____
_____
_____
_____
_____
_____

HOW DID THIS IMPACT / AFFECT YOU?

_____
_____
_____
_____
_____
_____

(IT'S TIME TO PASS IT ON)

> On the next page, decide who will receive your Act of Good and what you want to do for them.

WHO
WILL RECEIVE YOUR ACT OF GOOD?

It's time to decide who will receive your Act of Good. Choosing who you are going to do your Act of Good for makes deciding what you are going to do much easier.

- NEIGHBOR
- FRIEND
- STRANGER
- TEACHER
- CO-WORKER
- FAMILY MEMBER
- NEW ACQUAINTANCE
- _____ (OTHER)

(ONCE YOU DECIDE...)

TELL US WHY YOU CHOSE THIS PERSON

_____
_____
_____
_____

WHAT
ARE YOU GOING TO DO FOR THEM?

Explore the thoughts and questions below as you start to define / plan your Act Of Good. Remember that this is about making the person feel thought of, cared for, loved, noticed, remarkable, and accepted, so let that be your inspiration.

- Focus your thoughts on the person you chose.
- Reflect on your past conversations.
- What makes them smile?
- What do they enjoy?
- Do they have any wants, needs or goals?
- Would your time, talent or ability help them?
- Is it an activity?
- Is it a gift?
- Have you decided?
- Turn the page for final instructions on how to pass it on.

IT'S TIME TO DO THE 4TH ACT OF GOOD AND PASS IT ON.

Put the bookmark on the opening page of the next Act of Good before you give them the journal.

Look up this journal from time to time at ActsOfGood.com to find out where it is.

THANK YOU FOR BEING A PART OF THIS JOURNAL AND MAKING THE WORLD A BETTER PLACE!

SHARE YOUR EXPERIENCE

ACT
5

YOU ARE THE 5TH PERSON TO RECEIVE THIS JOURNAL

HERE'S HOW IT WORKS

This journal has been released into the world to create and inspire Acts of Good. Each journal is passed from one person to the next through an Act of Good, capturing the stories of where it goes, what it does and the lives touched along the way. It could have been given to millions of other people, yet here it lies in your hands. After all 12 Acts have been completed, this journal will be returned to its owner to share the stories of how you made the world a better place.

Follow the steps below to complete the next Act of Good:

STEP 1

CHECK-IN THIS JOURNAL

Go to: **ActsOfGood.com** and check this journal in. This lets everyone know where it is and allows you to track / follow where it goes after you pass it on.

(YOU CAN FIND THIS JOURNAL # IN THE FRONT OF THE BOOK)

STEP 2

WRITE IN THE JOURNAL

Over the next few pages, tell us a little about yourself and your experience.

STEP 3

PASS IT ON!

Complete the fifth Act of Good for someone, and give them this journal. How you choose to do so is up to you. Don't let rules, zip codes or actions limit your creativity.

(VISIT ActsOfGood.com IF YOU HAVE ANY QUESTIONS ABOUT HOW THIS WORKS)

TELL US ABOUT YOURSELF

M F
CIRCLE ONE
SEX

WRITE HERE
AGE

WHAT IS TODAY'S DATE?

_____ / _____ / _____
(MONTH)   (DAY)   (YEAR)

WHERE ARE YOU CURRENTLY IN THE WORLD?

_____ / _____ / _____
(CITY)   (STATE)   (COUNTRY)

WHAT ARE 3 THINGS THAT MAKE YOU THE HAPPIEST?

1. _____
2. _____
3. _____

HOW DO YOU DEFINE YOUR RELIGION?
(WE ASK THESE QUESTIONS ONLY TO CELEBRATE DIVERSITY, BUT FEEL FREE TO SKIP IF YOU DON'T FEEL LIKE ANSWERING.)

_____
_____

TELL US ABOUT YOUR EXPERIENCE

WHAT ACT OF GOOD WAS DONE FOR YOU?

_____
_____
_____
_____
_____
_____
_____
_____

HOW DID THIS IMPACT / AFFECT YOU?

_____
_____
_____
_____
_____
_____
_____

(IT'S TIME TO PASS IT ON)

On the next page, decide who will receive your Act of Good and what you want to do for them.

WHO
WILL RECEIVE YOUR ACT OF GOOD?

It's time to decide who will receive your Act of Good. Choosing who you are going to do your Act of Good for makes deciding what you are going to do much easier.

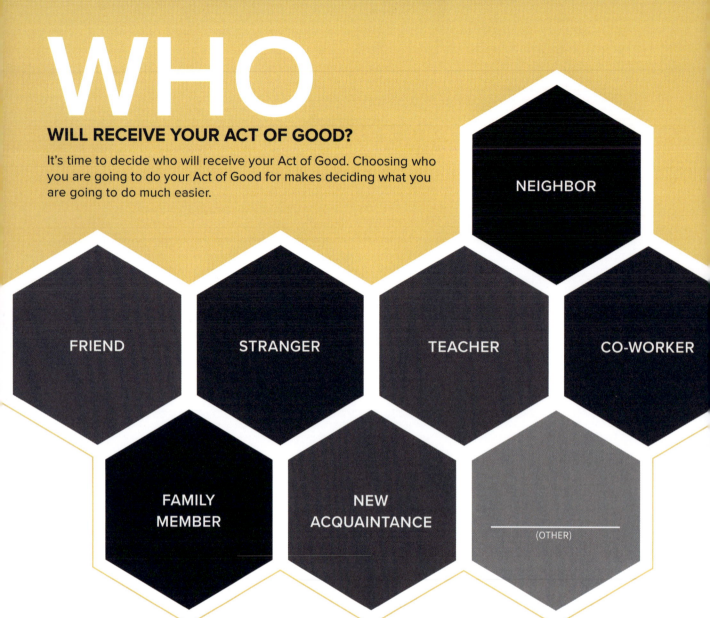

- NEIGHBOR
- FRIEND
- STRANGER
- TEACHER
- CO-WORKER
- FAMILY MEMBER
- NEW ACQUAINTANCE
- _____ (OTHER)

(ONCE YOU DECIDE...)
TELL US WHY YOU CHOSE THIS PERSON

_____
_____
_____
_____

WHAT
ARE YOU GOING TO DO FOR THEM?

Explore the thoughts and questions below as you start to define / plan your Act Of Good. Remember that this is about making the person feel thought of, cared for, loved, noticed, remarkable, and accepted, so let that be your inspiration.

- Focus your thoughts on the person you chose.
- Reflect on your past conversations.
- What makes them smile?
- What do they enjoy?
- Do they have any wants, needs or goals?
- Would your time, talent or ability help them?
- Is it an activity?
- Is it a gift?
- Have you decided?
- Turn the page for final instructions on how to pass it on.

YOU ARE THE 6TH PERSON TO RECEIVE THIS JOURNAL

HERE'S HOW IT WORKS

This journal has been released into the world to create and inspire Acts of Good. Each journal is passed from one person to the next through an Act of Good, capturing the stories of where it goes, what it does and the lives touched along the way. It could have been given to millions of other people, yet here it lies in your hands. After all 12 Acts have been completed, this journal will be returned to its owner to share the stories of how you made the world a better place.

Follow the steps below to complete the next Act of Good:

STEP 1

STEP 2

STEP 3

CHECK-IN THIS JOURNAL

Go to: **ActsOfGood.com** and check this journal in. This lets everyone know where it is and allows you to track / follow where it goes after you pass it on.

(YOU CAN FIND THIS JOURNAL # IN THE FRONT OF THE BOOK)

WRITE IN THE JOURNAL

Over the next few pages, tell us a little about yourself and your experience.

PASS IT ON!

Complete the sixth Act of Good for someone, and give them this journal. How you choose to do so is up to you. Don't let rules, zip codes or actions limit your creativity.

(VISIT ActsOfGood.com IF YOU HAVE ANY QUESTIONS ABOUT HOW THIS WORKS)

TELL US ABOUT YOURSELF

M F
CIRCLE ONE
SEX

WRITE HERE
AGE

WHAT IS TODAY'S DATE?

_____ / _____ / _____
(MONTH)   (DAY)   (YEAR)

WHERE ARE YOU CURRENTLY IN THE WORLD?

_____ / _____ / _____
(CITY)   (STATE)   (COUNTRY)

WHAT'S A "LOCAL" ___(ANYTHING)___ PEOPLE SHOULD KNOW ABOUT?
(AND WHY?)

_____
_____
_____

HOW DO YOU DEFINE YOUR POLITICAL AFFILIATION?
(WE ASK THESE QUESTIONS ONLY TO CELEBRATE DIVERSITY, BUT FEEL FREE TO SKIP IF YOU DON'T FEEL LIKE ANSWERING.)

_____
_____

TELL US ABOUT YOUR EXPERIENCE

WHAT ACT OF GOOD WAS DONE FOR YOU?

_____
_____
_____
_____
_____
_____
_____
_____

HOW DID THIS IMPACT / AFFECT YOU?

_____
_____
_____
_____
_____
_____
_____

(IT'S TIME TO PASS IT ON)

On the next page, decide who will receive your Act of Good and what you want to do for them.

WHO
WILL RECEIVE YOUR ACT OF GOOD?

It's time to decide who will receive your Act of Good. Choosing who you are going to do your Act of Good for makes deciding what you are going to do much easier.

- NEIGHBOR
- FRIEND
- STRANGER
- TEACHER
- CO-WORKER
- FAMILY MEMBER
- NEW ACQUAINTANCE
- _____ (OTHER)

(ONCE YOU DECIDE...)
TELL US WHY YOU CHOSE THIS PERSON

_____
_____
_____
_____

WHAT
ARE YOU GOING TO DO FOR THEM?

Explore the thoughts and questions below as you start to define / plan your Act Of Good. Remember that this is about making the person feel thought of, cared for, loved, noticed, remarkable, and accepted, so let that be your inspiration.

- Focus your thoughts on the person you chose.
- Reflect on your past conversations.
- What makes them smile?
- What do they enjoy?
- Do they have any wants, needs or goals?
- Would your time, talent or ability help them?
- Is it an activity?
- Is it a gift?
- Have you decided?
- Turn the page for final instructions on how to pass it on.

IT'S TIME TO DO THE 6ᵀᴴ ACT OF GOOD AND PASS IT ON.

Put the bookmark on the opening page of the next Act of Good before you give them the journal.

Look up this journal from time to time at ActsOfGood.com to find out where it is.

THANK YOU FOR BEING A PART OF THIS JOURNAL AND MAKING THE WORLD A BETTER PLACE!

SHARE YOUR EXPERIENCE

YOU ARE THE 7TH PERSON TO RECEIVE THIS JOURNAL

HERE'S HOW IT WORKS

This journal has been released into the world to create and inspire Acts of Good. Each journal is passed from one person to the next through an Act of Good, capturing the stories of where it goes, what it does and the lives touched along the way. It could have been given to millions of other people, yet here it lies in your hands. After all 12 Acts have been completed, this journal will be returned to its owner to share the stories of how you made the world a better place.

Follow the steps below to complete the next Act of Good:

 STEP 1

 STEP 2

 STEP 3

CHECK-IN THIS JOURNAL

Go to: **ActsOfGood.com** and check this journal in. This lets everyone know where it is and allows you to track / follow where it goes after you pass it on.

(YOU CAN FIND THIS JOURNAL # IN THE FRONT OF THE BOOK)

WRITE IN THE JOURNAL

Over the next few pages, tell us a little about yourself and your experience.

PASS IT ON!

Complete the seventh Act of Good for someone, and give them this journal. How you choose to do so is up to you. Don't let rules, zip codes or actions limit your creativity.

(VISIT ActsOfGood.com IF YOU HAVE ANY QUESTIONS ABOUT HOW THIS WORKS)

TELL US ABOUT YOURSELF

M F
CIRCLE ONE
SEX

WRITE HERE
AGE

WHAT IS TODAY'S DATE?

_____ / _____ / _____
(MONTH)   (DAY)   (YEAR)

WHERE ARE YOU CURRENTLY IN THE WORLD?

_____ / _____ / _____
(CITY)   (STATE)   (COUNTRY)

WHO DO YOU LOOK UP TO, AND WHY?
(PUBLIC FIGURE, SOMEONE YOU KNOW...)

_____

_____

_____

WHAT ARE YOUR GRANDPARENTS' ETHNICITIES?
(WE ASK THESE QUESTIONS ONLY TO CELEBRATE DIVERSITY, BUT FEEL FREE TO SKIP IF YOU DON'T FEEL LIKE ANSWERING.)

_____   _____
(DAD'S DAD)   (DAD'S MOM)

_____   _____
(MOM'S DAD)   (MOM'S MOM)

TELL US ABOUT YOUR EXPERIENCE

WHAT ACT OF GOOD WAS DONE FOR YOU?

_____
_____
_____
_____
_____
_____
_____
_____

HOW DID THIS IMPACT / AFFECT YOU?

_____
_____
_____
_____
_____
_____

(IT'S TIME TO PASS IT ON)

On the next page, decide who will receive your Act of Good and what you want to do for them.

WHO
WILL RECEIVE YOUR ACT OF GOOD?

It's time to decide who will receive your Act of Good. Choosing who you are going to do your Act of Good for makes deciding what you are going to do much easier.

- NEIGHBOR
- FRIEND
- STRANGER
- TEACHER
- CO-WORKER
- FAMILY MEMBER
- NEW ACQUAINTANCE
- _____ (OTHER)

(ONCE YOU DECIDE...)
TELL US WHY YOU CHOSE THIS PERSON

_____
_____
_____
_____

WHAT
ARE YOU GOING TO DO FOR THEM?

Explore the thoughts and questions below as you start to define / plan your Act Of Good. Remember that this is about making the person feel thought of, cared for, loved, noticed, remarkable, and accepted, so let that be your inspiration.

- Focus your thoughts on the person you chose.
- Reflect on your past conversations.
- What makes them smile?
- What do they enjoy?
- Do they have any wants, needs or goals?
- Would your time, talent or ability help them?
- Is it an activity?
- Is it a gift?
- Have you decided?
- Turn the page for final instructions on how to pass it on.

IT'S TIME TO DO THE 7TH ACT OF GOOD AND PASS IT ON.

Put the bookmark on the opening page of the next Act of Good before you give them the journal.

Look up this journal from time to time at ActsOfGood.com to find out where it is.

THANK YOU FOR BEING A PART OF THIS JOURNAL AND MAKING THE WORLD A BETTER PLACE!

SHARE YOUR EXPERIENCE

YOU ARE THE 8TH PERSON TO RECEIVE THIS JOURNAL

HERE'S HOW IT WORKS

This journal has been released into the world to create and inspire Acts of Good. Each journal is passed from one person to the next through an Act of Good, capturing the stories of where it goes, what it does and the lives touched along the way. It could have been given to millions of other people, yet here it lies in your hands. After all 12 Acts have been completed, this journal will be returned to its owner to share the stories of how you made the world a better place.

Follow the steps below to complete the next Act of Good:

STEP 1

CHECK-IN THIS JOURNAL

Go to: **ActsOfGood.com** and check this journal in. This lets everyone know where it is and allows you to track / follow where it goes after you pass it on.

(YOU CAN FIND THIS JOURNAL # IN THE FRONT OF THE BOOK)

STEP 2

WRITE IN THE JOURNAL

Over the next few pages, tell us a little about yourself and your experience.

STEP 3

PASS IT ON!

Complete the eighth Act of Good for someone, and give them this journal. How you choose to do so is up to you. Don't let rules, zip codes or actions limit your creativity.

(VISIT ActsOfGood.com IF YOU HAVE ANY QUESTIONS ABOUT HOW THIS WORKS)

TELL US ABOUT YOURSELF

M F
CIRCLE ONE
SEX

WRITE HERE
AGE

WHAT IS TODAY'S DATE?

_____ / _____ / _____
(MONTH)   (DAY)   (YEAR)

WHERE ARE YOU CURRENTLY IN THE WORLD?

_____ / _____ / _____
(CITY)   (STATE)   (COUNTRY)

WHAT ARE 3 THINGS THAT MAKE YOU THE HAPPIEST?

1. _____
2. _____
3. _____

HOW DO YOU DEFINE YOUR RELIGION?
(WE ASK THESE QUESTIONS ONLY TO CELEBRATE DIVERSITY, BUT FEEL FREE TO SKIP IF YOU DON'T FEEL LIKE ANSWERING.)

_____

_____

TELL US ABOUT YOUR EXPERIENCE

WHAT ACT OF GOOD WAS DONE FOR YOU?

_____
_____
_____
_____
_____
_____
_____
_____

HOW DID THIS IMPACT / AFFECT YOU?

_____
_____
_____
_____
_____
_____
_____

(IT'S TIME TO PASS IT ON)

On the next page, decide who will receive your Act of Good and what you want to do for them.

WHO
WILL RECEIVE YOUR ACT OF GOOD?

It's time to decide who will receive your Act of Good. Choosing who you are going to do your Act of Good for makes deciding what you are going to do much easier.

- NEIGHBOR
- FRIEND
- STRANGER
- TEACHER
- CO-WORKER
- FAMILY MEMBER
- NEW ACQUAINTANCE
- _____ (OTHER)

(ONCE YOU DECIDE...)
TELL US WHY YOU CHOSE THIS PERSON

_____
_____
_____
_____

WHAT

ARE YOU GOING TO DO FOR THEM?

Explore the thoughts and questions below as you start to define / plan your Act Of Good. Remember that this is about making the person feel thought of, cared for, loved, noticed, remarkable, and accepted, so let that be your inspiration.

- Focus your thoughts on the person you chose.
- Reflect on your past conversations.
- What makes them smile?
- What do they enjoy?
- Do they have any wants, needs or goals?
- Would your time, talent or ability help them?
- Is it an activity?
- Is it a gift?
- Have you decided?
- Turn the page for final instructions on how to pass it on.

IT'S TIME TO DO THE 8TH ACT OF GOOD AND PASS IT ON.

Put the bookmark on the opening page of the next Act of Good before you give them the journal.

Look up this journal from time to time at ActsOfGood.com to find out where it is.

THANK YOU FOR BEING A PART OF THIS JOURNAL AND MAKING THE WORLD A BETTER PLACE!

SHARE YOUR EXPERIENCE

ACT 9

YOU ARE THE 9TH PERSON TO RECEIVE THIS JOURNAL

HERE'S HOW IT WORKS

This journal has been released into the world to create and inspire Acts of Good. Each journal is passed from one person to the next through an Act of Good, capturing the stories of where it goes, what it does and the lives touched along the way. It could have been given to millions of other people, yet here it lies in your hands. After all 12 Acts have been completed, this journal will be returned to its owner to share the stories of how you made the world a better place.

Follow the steps below to complete the next Act of Good:

STEP 1

CHECK-IN THIS JOURNAL

Go to: **ActsOfGood.com** and check this journal in. This lets everyone know where it is and allows you to track / follow where it goes after you pass it on.

(YOU CAN FIND THIS JOURNAL # IN THE FRONT OF THE BOOK)

STEP 2

WRITE IN THE JOURNAL

Over the next few pages, tell us a little about yourself and your experience.

STEP 3

PASS IT ON!

Complete the ninth Act of Good for someone, and give them this journal. How you choose to do so is up to you. Don't let rules, zip codes or actions limit your creativity.

(VISIT ActsOfGood.com IF YOU HAVE ANY QUESTIONS ABOUT HOW THIS WORKS)

TELL US ABOUT YOURSELF

SEX — M F (CIRCLE ONE)

AGE — WRITE HERE

WHAT IS TODAY'S DATE?
___ / ___ / ___
(MONTH) (DAY) (YEAR)

WHERE ARE YOU CURRENTLY IN THE WORLD?
___ / ___ / ___
(CITY) (STATE) (COUNTRY)

WHAT'S A "LOCAL" __(ANYTHING)__ PEOPLE SHOULD KNOW ABOUT?
(AND WHY?)

_____
_____

HOW DO YOU DEFINE YOUR POLITICAL AFFILIATION?
(WE ASK THESE QUESTIONS ONLY TO CELEBRATE DIVERSITY, BUT FEEL FREE TO SKIP IF YOU DON'T FEEL LIKE ANSWERING.)

_____
_____

TELL US ABOUT YOUR EXPERIENCE

WHAT ACT OF GOOD WAS DONE FOR YOU?

_____
_____
_____
_____
_____
_____
_____
_____

HOW DID THIS IMPACT / AFFECT YOU?

_____
_____
_____
_____
_____
_____
_____

(IT'S TIME TO PASS IT ON)

On the next page, decide who will receive your Act of Good and what you want to do for them.

WHO

WILL RECEIVE YOUR ACT OF GOOD?

It's time to decide who will receive your Act of Good. Choosing who you are going to do your Act of Good for makes deciding what you are going to do much easier.

- NEIGHBOR
- FRIEND
- STRANGER
- TEACHER
- CO-WORKER
- FAMILY MEMBER
- NEW ACQUAINTANCE
- _____ (OTHER)

(ONCE YOU DECIDE...)

TELL US WHY YOU CHOSE THIS PERSON

_____
_____
_____
_____

WHAT
ARE YOU GOING TO DO FOR THEM?

Explore the thoughts and questions below as you start to define / plan your Act Of Good. Remember that this is about making the person feel thought of, cared for, loved, noticed, remarkable, and accepted, so let that be your inspiration.

- Focus your thoughts on the person you chose.
- Reflect on your past conversations.
- What makes them smile?
- What do they enjoy?
- Do they have any wants, needs or goals?
- Would your time, talent or ability help them?
- Is it an activity?
- Is it a gift?
- Have you decided?
- Turn the page for final instructions on how to pass it on.

IT'S TIME TO DO THE 9TH ACT OF GOOD AND PASS IT ON.

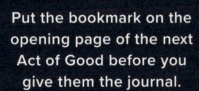

Put the bookmark on the opening page of the next Act of Good before you give them the journal.

Look up this journal from time to time at ActsOfGood.com to find out where it is.

THANK YOU FOR BEING A PART OF THIS JOURNAL AND MAKING THE WORLD A BETTER PLACE!

SHARE YOUR EXPERIENCE

YOU ARE THE 10TH PERSON TO RECEIVE THIS JOURNAL

HERE'S HOW IT WORKS

This journal has been released into the world to create and inspire Acts of Good. Each journal is passed from one person to the next through an Act of Good, capturing the stories of where it goes, what it does and the lives touched along the way. It could have been given to millions of other people, yet here it lies in your hands. After all 12 Acts have been completed, this journal will be returned to its owner to share the stories of how you made the world a better place.

Follow the steps below to complete the next Act of Good:

STEP 1

STEP 2

STEP 3

CHECK-IN THIS JOURNAL

WRITE IN THE JOURNAL

PASS IT ON!

Go to: **ActsOfGood.com** and check this journal in. This lets everyone know where it is and allows you to track / follow where it goes after you pass it on.

(YOU CAN FIND THIS JOURNAL # IN THE FRONT OF THE BOOK)

Over the next few pages, tell us a little about yourself and your experience.

Complete the tenth Act of Good for someone, and give them this journal. How you choose to do so is up to you. Don't let rules, zip codes or actions limit your creativity.

(VISIT ActsOfGood.com IF YOU HAVE ANY QUESTIONS ABOUT HOW THIS WORKS)

TELL US ABOUT YOURSELF

M F
CIRCLE ONE
SEX

WRITE HERE
AGE

WHAT IS TODAY'S DATE?

_____ / _____ / _____
(MONTH)   (DAY)   (YEAR)

WHERE ARE YOU CURRENTLY IN THE WORLD?

_____ / _____ / _____
(CITY)   (STATE)   (COUNTRY)

WHO DO YOU LOOK UP TO, AND WHY?
(PUBLIC FIGURE, SOMEONE YOU KNOW...)

_____
_____
_____

WHAT ARE YOUR GRANDPARENTS' ETHNICITIES?
(WE ASK THESE QUESTIONS ONLY TO CELEBRATE DIVERSITY, BUT FEEL FREE TO SKIP IF YOU DON'T FEEL LIKE ANSWERING.)

_____   _____
(DAD'S DAD)   (DAD'S MOM)

_____   _____
(MOM'S DAD)   (MOM'S MOM)

TELL US ABOUT YOUR EXPERIENCE

WHAT ACT OF GOOD WAS DONE FOR YOU?

_____
_____
_____
_____
_____
_____
_____
_____

HOW DID THIS IMPACT / AFFECT YOU?

_____
_____
_____
_____
_____
_____
_____

(IT'S TIME TO PASS IT ON)

On the next page, decide who will receive your Act of Good and what you want to do for them.

WHO
WILL RECEIVE YOUR ACT OF GOOD?

It's time to decide who will receive your Act of Good. Choosing who you are going to do your Act of Good for makes deciding what you are going to do much easier.

- NEIGHBOR
- FRIEND
- STRANGER
- TEACHER
- CO-WORKER
- FAMILY MEMBER
- NEW ACQUAINTANCE
- _____ (OTHER)

(ONCE YOU DECIDE...)
TELL US WHY YOU CHOSE THIS PERSON

_____
_____
_____
_____

WHAT
ARE YOU GOING TO DO FOR THEM?

Explore the thoughts and questions below as you start to define / plan your Act Of Good. Remember that this is about making the person feel thought of, cared for, loved, noticed, remarkable, and accepted, so let that be your inspiration.

- Focus your thoughts on the person you chose.
- Reflect on your past conversations.
- What makes them smile?
- What do they enjoy?
- Do they have any wants, needs or goals?
- Would your time, talent or ability help them?
- Is it an activity?
- Is it a gift?
- Have you decided?
- Turn the page for final instructions on how to pass it on.

IT'S TIME TO DO THE 10TH ACT OF GOOD AND PASS IT ON.

Put the bookmark on the opening page of the next Act of Good before you give them the journal.

Look up this journal from time to time at ActsOfGood.com to find out where it is.

THANK YOU FOR BEING A PART OF THIS JOURNAL AND MAKING THE WORLD A BETTER PLACE!

SHARE YOUR EXPERIENCE

ACT 11

YOU ARE THE 11TH PERSON TO RECEIVE THIS JOURNAL

HERE'S HOW IT WORKS

This journal has been released into the world to create and inspire Acts of Good. Each journal is passed from one person to the next through an Act of Good, capturing the stories of where it goes, what it does and the lives touched along the way. It could have been given to millions of other people, yet here it lies in your hands. After all 12 Acts have been completed, this journal will be returned to its owner to share the stories of how you made the world a better place.

Follow the steps below to complete the next Act of Good:

STEP 1

CHECK-IN THIS JOURNAL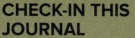

Go to: **ActsOfGood.com** and check this journal in. This lets everyone know where it is and allows you to track / follow where it goes after you pass it on.

(YOU CAN FIND THIS JOURNAL # IN THE FRONT OF THE BOOK)

STEP 2

WRITE IN THE JOURNAL

Over the next few pages, tell us a little about yourself and your experience.

STEP 3

PASS IT ON!

Complete the eleventh Act of Good for someone, and give them this journal. How you choose to do so is up to you. Don't let rules, zip codes or actions limit your creativity.

(VISIT ActsOfGood.com IF YOU HAVE ANY QUESTIONS ABOUT HOW THIS WORKS)

TELL US ABOUT YOURSELF

M F
CIRCLE ONE
SEX

WRITE HERE
AGE

WHAT IS TODAY'S DATE?
_____ / _____ / _____
(MONTH)   (DAY)   (YEAR)

WHERE ARE YOU CURRENTLY IN THE WORLD?
_____ / _____ / _____
(CITY)   (STATE)   (COUNTRY)

WHAT ARE 3 THINGS THAT MAKE YOU THE HAPPIEST?

1. _____
2. _____
3. _____

HOW DO YOU DEFINE YOUR RELIGION?
(WE ASK THESE QUESTIONS ONLY TO CELEBRATE DIVERSITY, BUT FEEL FREE TO SKIP IF YOU DON'T FEEL LIKE ANSWERING.)

_____
_____

TELL US ABOUT YOUR EXPERIENCE

WHAT ACT OF GOOD WAS DONE FOR YOU?

_____
_____
_____
_____
_____
_____
_____
_____

HOW DID THIS IMPACT / AFFECT YOU?

_____
_____
_____
_____
_____
_____
_____

(IT'S TIME TO PASS IT ON)

On the next page, decide who will receive your Act of Good and what you want to do for them.

WHO
WILL RECEIVE YOUR ACT OF GOOD?

It's time to decide who will receive your Act of Good. Choosing who you are going to do your Act of Good for makes deciding what you are going to do much easier.

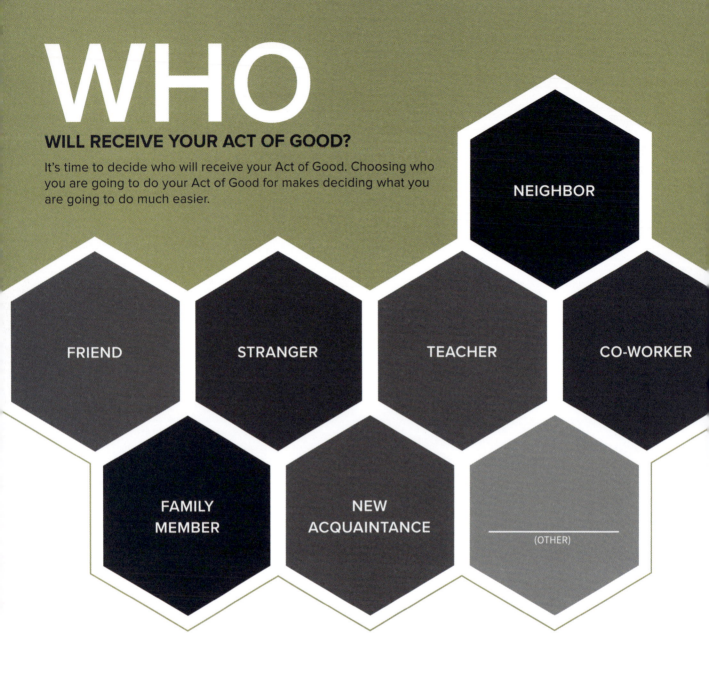

- NEIGHBOR
- FRIEND
- STRANGER
- TEACHER
- CO-WORKER
- FAMILY MEMBER
- NEW ACQUAINTANCE
- _____ (OTHER)

(ONCE YOU DECIDE...)
TELL US WHY YOU CHOSE THIS PERSON

_____
_____
_____
_____

WHAT

ARE YOU GOING TO DO FOR THEM?

Explore the thoughts and questions below as you start to define / plan your Act Of Good. Remember that this is about making the person feel thought of, cared for, loved, noticed, remarkable, and accepted, so let that be your inspiration.

- Focus your thoughts on the person you chose.
- Reflect on your past conversations.
- What makes them smile?
- What do they enjoy?
- Do they have any wants, needs or goals?
- Would your time, talent or ability help them?
- Is it an activity?
- Is it a gift?
- Have you decided?
- Turn the page for final instructions on how to pass it on.

IT'S TIME TO DO THE 11TH ACT OF GOOD AND PASS IT ON.

Put the bookmark on the opening page of the next Act of Good before you give them the journal.

Look up this journal from time to time at ActsOfGood.com to find out where it is.

THANK YOU FOR BEING A PART OF THIS JOURNAL AND MAKING THE WORLD A BETTER PLACE!

SHARE YOUR EXPERIENCE

ACT
12

YOU ARE THE 12TH PERSON TO RECEIVE THIS JOURNAL

HERE'S HOW IT WORKS

This journal has been released into the world to create and inspire Acts of Good. Each journal has been passed from one person to the next through an Act of Good, capturing the stories of where it went, what it did and the lives it touched along the way. It could have been given to millions of other people, yet here it lies in your hands. Since you are the last person to receive this journal, it is your job to complete the final Act of Good and return the journal to the original owner.

Follow the steps below to complete the final Act of Good:

STEP 1

STEP 2

STEP 3

CHECK-IN THIS JOURNAL

Go to: **ActsOfGood.com** and check this journal in. This lets everyone know where it is and will automatically send you a prepaid envelope in the mail to return this journal to the original owner.

(YOU CAN FIND THIS JOURNAL # IN THE FRONT OF THE BOOK)

WRITE IN THE JOURNAL

Over the next few pages, tell us a little about yourself and your experience.

MAIL THE JOURNAL BACK TO US!

It's easy! Once you receive our prepaid envelope, follow the instructions to mail it back. This will complete the final Act of Good!

(VISIT ActsOfGood.com IF YOU HAVE ANY QUESTIONS ABOUT HOW THIS WORKS)

TELL US ABOUT YOURSELF

M F
CIRCLE ONE
SEX

WRITE HERE
AGE

WHAT IS TODAY'S DATE?

_____ / _____ / _____
(MONTH)   (DAY)   (YEAR)

WHERE ARE YOU CURRENTLY IN THE WORLD?

_____ / _____ / _____
(CITY)   (STATE)   (COUNTRY)

WHAT'S A "LOCAL" ___(ANYTHING)___ PEOPLE SHOULD KNOW ABOUT?
(AND WHY?)

_____
_____
_____

HOW DO YOU DEFINE YOUR POLITICAL AFFILIATION?
(WE ASK THESE QUESTIONS ONLY TO CELEBRATE DIVERSITY, BUT FEEL FREE TO SKIP IF YOU DON'T FEEL LIKE ANSWERING.)

_____
_____

TELL US ABOUT YOUR EXPERIENCE

WHAT ACT OF GOOD WAS DONE FOR YOU?

_____
_____
_____
_____
_____
_____
_____

HOW DID THIS IMPACT / AFFECT YOU?

_____
_____
_____
_____
_____
_____

(IT'S TIME TO RETURN IT)

On the next page, follow the instructions to return the journal.

IT'S TIME TO RETURN IT!

 STEP 1

RECEIVE THE PREPAID ENVELOPE.

If you haven't already, go to ActsOfGood.com and check this journal in. This lets everyone know where it is and we will automatically mail you a prepaid envelope to return this journal to the original owner.

 STEP 2

PROPERLY SEAL THE JOURNAL IN THE ENVELOPE.

Place the journal in the prepaid envelope, and seal it shut by removing the adhesive strip and folding it over to secure the package.

 STEP 3

PUT IT IN THE MAIL!

It is now time to do the final Act of Good and simply put it in the mail.

THANK YOU FOR BEING A PART OF THIS JOURNAL AND MAKING THE WORLD A BETTER PLACE!

SHARE YOUR EXPERIENCE

Terms and Conditions:
All content written or collected in this journal is owned by Inspire Good Publishing Co. By writing in this journal, you grant a perpetual, irrevocable, fully paid and royalty-free license to use all written or other works created by you (collectively, "Content") without restrictions. The license shall include, without limitation, the irrevocable right to reproduce, prepare derivative works, combine with other works, alter, translate, distribute copies, display, perform, reduce to practice, utilize in its business, license the content, and all rights therein, in the name of Inspire Good Publishing Co.

By writing in and participatiting with this journal, you hereby irrevocably release and forever discharge Inspire Good Publishing Co. and all of our officers, directors, owners, employees, agents, advertisers, sponsors, information providers, franchisees, affiliates, partners, and licensors (collectively, "Inspire Good Publishing Co. Parties") and hold harmless Inspire Good Publishing Co. Parties from and against any and all liability, losses, costs, and expenses, including attorneys' fees, incurred by any Inspire Good Publishing Co. Party in connection with any claim, including, but not limited to, claims for defamation, safety, violation of rights of publicity or privacy, copyright infringement, or trademark infringements, all actions, causes of actions, claims, damages, liabilities and demands, whether absolute or contingent of any nature whatsoever, which you now have or hereafter can, shall or may have against Inspire Good Publishing Co. and its affiliates and subsidiaries or their respective successors arising out of Inspire Good Publishing Co. and The Acts of Good Journal.

Copyright © 2017 Inspire Good Publishing Co. | All Rights Reserved | Printed in China | ISBN 978-1-945966-00-2

CREATIVE THANKS

We have been so fortunate to collaborate with these incredibly talented photographers, creatives and artists to create a beautiful atmosphere for these Acts of Good to live. The images in this volume invite experience, encourage participation and evoke imagination into a world of good.

Michelle Park
www.michelleparkphotography.com
Instagram: @trainsandplanes
Photo(s): Act 4 (2nd Image); Act 8 (2nd Image)

Gen.One.Three Photography
www.genonethreephotography.com
Instagram: @gen.one.three
Photo(s): Act 7 (1st Image)

Tri Sanguanbun
Instagram: @tri_11
Photo(s): Act 3 (2nd Image)

Samuel Mahtani
www.samuelmahtani.com
Instagram: @samuelmahtani
Photo(s): Act 1 (2nd Image); Act 6 (1st Image); Act 10 (2nd Image)

Sarah Sweeney
www.sarahsweeney.co
Instagram: @sarahsweenyco
Photo(s): Act 1 (1st Image); Act 2 (2nd Image); Act 3 (1st Image); Act 11 (1st Image); Act 12 (1st Image)

Trisikh Sanguanbun
Instagram: @ts_xiv
Photo(s): Act 5 (1st Image); Act 7 (2nd Image)

Evan Skoczenski
www.evanskoczenski.com
Instagram: @evanskoczenski
Photo(s): Act 2 (1st Image); Act 5 (2nd Image); Act 12 (2nd Image)

Adam Benton
www.adam-benton.com
Photo(s): Act 9 (1st Image); Act 10 (1st Image)

Saskia Wilson
www.saskiawilson.com
Instagram: @saskiawilson
Photo(s): Act 8 (1st Image)

Brady Davidson
www.bradydavidson.com
Instagram: @bradydavidson
Photo(s): Act 4 (1st Image); Act 6 (2nd Image); Act 9 (2nd Image); Act 11 (2nd Image)

#GIVE G

This journal was created to inspire Acts Of Good. A tangible book released into the world to capture the stories of the lives touched along the way. Each journal starts as a blank canvas, passed from one person to the next through an Act of Good, uniquely documenting the path, impact and effect it has on the world before it is returned to you as a completed manuscript of how you made the world a better place.